Giving Birth To An Anointed Ministry

Birthing God's Vision For Your Life

Bishop Edward Wilson

LIVING WORD MINISTRIES, INC.,
DIAMOND IN THE ROUGH PUBLICATIONS

GIVING BIRTH TO AN ANOINTED MINISTRY
By Pastor Edward Wilson

ISBN: 978-0-6151-8015-1

Diamond In The Rough Publications in Association with
Living Word Ministries, Inc.

For information, address Living Word Ministries, Inc.
4 Concord Drive, P.O. Box 695 Williamstown, NJ 08094

This book is dedicated to the praise and glory of my Lord and Saviour Jesus Christ, the God of all flesh, who lives moves and breathes in me.

It is also lovingly dedicated to my wife Ann, my mother Ruth, my daughter Amber, the memory of the work of District Elder George Mayfield, the entire Mt. Zion church family, and all who have touched my life and helped me be the person I am today.

To God be the glory for the things he has done.

Contents

FOREWORD

When I initially set out to build a church for the Lord, I was not remotely aware of the sacrifice and the struggle it would take to successfully do this kind of work for God. I remember the call of God on my life. I even remember the struggle to accept Him calling me, and my wife into the Pastoral Ministry. I knew that this was a big challenge, but I could never have anticipated the struggles that lay ahead.

At the time God called me to leave the comfort of the church where I had been saved and grew up as a Christian, I had a great deal of compassion for the job our pastor was doing and even more so for those who had gone before him. But, it was not until I moved out and began striving to build a ministry to the glory of God, that I got a real appreciation for what it takes to carve out a ministry.

I have often since said, that anybody can attend the church of your choice, but it takes a special gift of the grace of God working in your life to carve out a ministry. There are no specific guidebooks for every individual circumstance. Every situation is somewhat different.

Because each person is a unique individual, each circumstance will be unique.

What I hope to do in this book, is inspire those who would build and those who are building a ministry of any kind; whether it be music, teaching, preaching, pastoring or any other ministry, to continue doing what God has ordained for you to do, knowing, that *"You are Pregnant With An Anointed Ministry"*. Whatever God has ordained for you through foreknowledge from before the foundation of the world he will do, if we let him.

The Bible says in Isaiah 66:9 *"Shall I bring to the birth, and not cause to bring forth?..."* Philippians 1:6 says: *"Being confident of this very thing, that he which hath begun a good work in you will perform it until the day of Jesus Christ:..."*

From the moment you were saved, God impregnated you with an anointed ministry. But it will take the fullness of God's time to bring your ministry to life. Throughout this process you will go through a number of growth phases. The more you understand about the growth phases and how to handle them, the more inspired you will be as you allow God to birth your ministry.

The First Tri-Mester

"Before I formed thee in the belly I knew thee; and before thou camest forth out of the womb I sanctified thee, and I ordained thee a prophet unto the nations

Jeremiah 1:5

Pregnant With An Anointed Ministry

I have found that the book of Isaiah is one of the most inspiring books of the Bible. Within its pages are found a great number of outstanding Bible truths, doctrinal statements and revelations about the God of Abraham, Isaac and Jacob. But one of the most inspiring scriptures I found in the book of Isaiah is in chapter 66 and verse 8 which reads: *"Who hath heard such a thing? who hath seen such things? Shall the earth be made to bring forth in one day? Or shall a nation be born at once? for as soon as Zion travailed, she brought forth her children..."*

I guess I found this scripture inspiring because, at that time in my life when I read that verse, I was a pastor struggling to give birth to a ministry that God had impregnated me with. I had read this scripture numerous times. I had even heard ministers preach about it. My former pastor District Elder Mayfield, and the saints at Pentecostal Bridegroom Church had instilled this scripture in me when they talked to me and other saints about being filled with the gift of the Holy Spirit. But, it never had such meaning as it did on this occasion. I had been seeking the Lord's guidance in completing a sermon series that he had placed on my heart. At church we were in the process of building a new sanctuary. The process had been somewhat slow, nothing seemed to be going as planned. The financing took longer than we had expected. The various government approvals seemed to take longer than normal, and I was beginning to wonder what was wrong. As I continued to seek God for the completion to the series I had been working on, God spoke a word into my spirit and told me to preach a sermon about the travail of childbirth. Immediately He dropped the scripture from Isaiah 66:8 into my spirit. I kept hearing this scripture echoing in my spirit, especially the latter clause, *"...for as soon as Zion travailed, she brought forth her children..."*

I prepared the message with enthusiasm, knowing that God had inspired me to preach it. Its one thing to prepare a word from a systematic schedule, but its an entirely different thing to prepare a totally God inspired sermon. I finished this particular message with no problem. There was no real struggle in developing the outline. The structure seemed to come naturally. I could not wait for Sunday, I was ready to preach this God inspired message.

Sunday mornings were usually very busy for me, and the Sunday that I was to preach this message was no different. We were at that time having services at a local catering facility. During this time I would get up every Sunday, cart the audio equipment over to the catering hall, get things set up and hurry back home to pick up my wife and daughter. On this Sunday morning as I was making my way home, while sitting at a traffic light, the Lord spoke again to my spirit and said; "Tell the people, Don't abort your baby [ministry]!" My first reaction was Lord, I didn't prepare to speak from that subject. Now I'm like any God inspired preacher, I don't mind changing the subject if God is in it. But on this morning the Lord said, use the outline you have, just change the title.

At 11 O'clock when I stood up to deliver this God inspired message with the new title, I told the congregation the following words. "God told me to tell you, Don't Abort Your Ministry". Then God inspired me to ask them to proclaim to their neighbor that they were pregnant with an anointed ministry. Suddenly so many things began to become clear to me. All the problems, all the struggle, all the trials that we had been going through, were a part of a birthing process. I began to realize that within each and every one of the Born Again children of God is an anointed ministry. I began to realize that many times the struggles of this life are simply the toil of pregnancy and the travail of childbirth. It is a lesson we learn so well from the caterpillar. Within the cocoon of the caterpillar is the beauty of the butterfly. It is the struggle of the caterpillar, as it strives to come out of the cocoon that makes its wings strong enough to fly. We cannot help the caterpillar to exit the cocoon, it must travail on its own, depending only upon the divine mercy, grace and strength of the God who has given it life. It must learn that there is another side to struggle. We like the caterpillar, must learn that if we are going to be able to fly then we must have our wings strengthened through struggle, toil and travail. For as soon as Zion shall travail she will bring forth her children. So then, travail is a natural part of growth. What is travail to the child of God? Travail represents lessons to be learned through experience. And it is the experiences that we encounter that properly prepare us for ministry. I once took a class in public speaking from The Dale Carnegie Schools. One of the things I remember most about the course was that the instructor said, that a speaker must speak or talk about things that you have earned the right to talk about. The best preacher in the world will be the one who has experienced things that help to make his or her preaching complete or full. I believe the best singer is the one who doesn't simply sing lyrics that have been written but one who sings lyrics based on experiences that have molded and shaped their character. These experiences cause the preacher to preach from the heart and the singer to not only use the vocal gift of God but give a heartfelt expression of the enduring hope and joy of a life shaped through experiences guided by the hand of God.

Pregnant And Unaware

It is interesting to note that the vast majority of the saints of God may not even be aware that God has impregnated them with an anointed ministry. Many times we can become very comfortable being "just" another member of a church. It may be that after having been saved we involve ourselves with the normal day to day struggles of life, and never give a second thought to the fact that after salvation God calls all of us to a life of ministry in one area or another. For many of the saints of God we go on with our lives, coming to church every Sunday, totally unaware of our spiritual pregnancy. Someone once told us of a young teenage child who spent nine months pregnant and unaware. She went to school as normal, took gym and even participated in sporting activities. This young lady never gave a thought to having prenatal care or even taking additional vitamins because she was unaware that she was pregnant. Even her parents were unaware of her pregnancy, They thought she was just gaining weight since most of her family were rather large people. It was not until she began to travail in pain that they realized that something was happening. To their surprise, she was pregnant. I have found that many of the people of God are in the same situation as this young lady was, pregnant but unaware. And because we continue with our lives going on doing what we are use to doing, no one else recognizes that there is something going on inside. They see us on Sunday morning, and we give them the traditional greeting of Praise the Lord. We continue to sing on the choir. We haven't stopped working the altar. We still clean the church bathrooms and polish the pews. We cook the food and serve the pastor. We carry the man of God's briefcase and help him change his clothes. We still shout or dance in the spirit and take joy in every aspect of the church service. But, we are unaware of our pregnancy, and because everything looks normal the church is unaware also.

I have no problem with "Mega Churches", but it is possible for your ministry to be swallowed up by your church. Mega Churches are popular and their is no denying that God is doing something in our larger churches. But every child of God should always strive to know their place and fulfill their ministry in the Kingdom of God. We should never despise a small fellowship of believers. It may be in a small ministry in some remote unheard of place that God chooses to fully use your spiritual gifts and talents. Remember God sent Philip the evangelist to a desert place to minister to one soul who was reading from God's holy writ. Many a small church would hold in high esteem one organist to play on Sunday and help build their ministry. You can either be a blessing in the small ministry or be one of 7 or 8 organist in a large one. You can wait on your turn to direct the 200 voice choir or you can allow God to use your talent on the 15 voice choir at the small church on the corner; bringing them to musical levels they only dreamed they could achieve. You can wait for your chance to preach in your home pulpit or you can find a corner, a park or a local radio station and let God begin to give birth to the ministry within.

As people of God, we need to be fully aware of the fact, that God did not only call and impregnate the great men and women who we see on television and hear on radio. But God gives each and every baptized, born again believer a job or ministry. If your ministry is to clean the church, pray over every pew. If your ministry is ushering, which I believe is one of the most important ministries in the church; pray for an anointing to greet and minister to the people of God. Begin asking God for wisdom and discernment, that you may give birth to a ministry of greeting and service like none before you. I encourage every person who has been told that you couldn't hold a note if you were carrying it in a bucket. It's a new day now, and the anointing will make the difference in your voice. If God has impregnated you with the ministry of song, your old life and voice is not an issue any longer. Go, get on the choir, pray, take voice lessons and struggle to birth the music ministry that God has placed within you. I remember so well sitting in Willingboro, New Jersey with a friend of mine; listening to him tell me the story of his desire to play a musical instrument, to be specific the piano and organ. He would go to the church and get on the piano and bang on the keys. His playing was so bad, he told me, that some folks in the congregation would ask him to play the piano during church service just so they could laugh at his playing. Unfettered by their laughter he continued to play, banging away at the keys day and night struggling to learn this instrument. He never took music lessons, but only believed that through prayer, God would *Anoint* him to play. God truly did anoint my friend to play the piano and the organ also. He learned to play so well that he became one of the most sought after organist in the tri-state Pennsylvania area. This great man of God later inspired and help train his son and nephew who are now some of the most well known keyboard players in the world. This man was my friend Deacon Thomas Ford Sr.. Who did he inspire? His son Kenny Ford and his nephew Steven Ford. Steven Ford has played for such notable groups as the Winans, Richard Smallwood and Vanessa Bell Armstrong. Because of his great talent as a musician, Deacon Ford became known to many keyboard artists as "The Maestro".

I have often told our congregation that, "Great people were not always great". Dr. Martin Luther King Jr., one of the greatest men of our day at age three was just little Martin, or maybe his mother only called him Junior. While sitting on the pew of his church as a young teenager; I can believe that to some degree he was unaware of the greatness that was already within him. Reverend Jesse Jackson was probably unaware of being pregnant with the Rainbow Coalition during his early years prior to the civil rights movement. No, great people were not always great, but somewhere along the line, great people begin to look inside themselves. They begin to evaluate their life; where they are, where they're going and what God's purpose is for them. It is out of this kind of introspective evaluation that we begin to realize that there is a burning desire within the depths of our soul to do something more. A burning desire to have an impact, to make a difference.

I believe that it is important for every child of God to take a look on the inside. Evaluate yourself and ask God for divine guidance into your purpose. As you do this I believe a burning desire for the area of ministry that God has for you will begin to swell up within your spirit. As you seek God's face, you will not be able to contain the longing to give birth to the ministry that has been set aside for you. Once you gain guidance from God as to your purpose, ask him for direction, that you may know how to get to your destination. The road may not be easy, but then most worthwhile things aren't. Remember butterflies are born through struggle. And, it is in struggling that a butterfly's wings develop strength. If you are going to soar in your ministry, there will be a certain degree of struggle. We must remember that our Lord and Saviour knows just how much you need and can bear. If we stay the course and endure hardness as a good soldier, we will realize that at the end of struggle there is victory.

Spontaneous Abortion

It has been said that as many as three fourths of human conceptions are *spontaneously aborted.* Spontaneous abortion occurs when the embryo fails to develop. Most spontaneous abortions occur before the woman's pregnancy can be confirmed.

I believe that the same is true of the ministries that we all carry within us. It is a fact that the devil is in no way looking forward to the child of God fulfilling the specific ministry that God has placed within their hands. The Bible says that "The thief cometh not, but for to steal, and to kill and to destroy:..." Satan's desire is to keep your ministry from ever coming to fruition, and what better way to do this than to cause it to abort in its beginning stages. There is probably no time that the embryo is more vulnerable than in the early stages of pregnancy. Likewise, the ministry that lay within the child of God is at its most vulnerable point when it is just a small yearning within the heart of the believer. It is at this time, in the early stages of birthing our ministry, that many of the people of God are somewhat unsure. We often question the mind of God and we wonder if what we are feeling is really God or our own desire to be like someone that we have seen or heard. We often wonder if we are simply being influenced by some of the popular men and women of God and not God Himself. This is when the devil comes and tries to destroy the dreamer and the dream. This is the time that the devil tries to kill the vision with the visionary. It is in these moments of uncertainty that we must do as Moses did and seek the face of God. When God is making you aware of the ministry which has been placed within your hands, there is no better place to be than in the presence of God. Only God can provide the spiritual nutrients necessary to bring you past this very critical stage in the development of your ministry. If you stay to yourself and depend on your own intellect or feelings you may miss the mind and will of God for your life. In the beginning stages of the call of God on my life to the pastorate, I questioned whether or not God had called me to this very difficult office. Those who were my senior seemed so much more qualified than myself. They were better Bible scholars. They had been saved longer. Many of them had been preachers long before I came to the Pentecostal church. I remember on one occasion, it was brought to my attention that someone had found out that I felt called to the pastoral ministry. Their reaction was that of laughter. In like manner, Sanballat the Horonite, and Tobiah the servant, and Geshem the Arabian laughed at the Idea that God had ordained Nehemiah to rebuild the walls of Jerusalem. But the Bible says that Nehemiah understood that the God of heaven would prosper him and his associates to do the will of God. As you could imagine, if I had not acted with the same strength of Nehemiah, if I had let their folly take root in my spirit, the devil could have used it to cause the seed of doubt to choke out the ministry God had planted within me. But, in the midst of laughter and criticism, the word of God, in the book of Isaiah chapter 55 verse 8 rang true and clear in my mind. "For my thoughts are not your thoughts, neither are your ways my ways, saith the Lord..." I am so glad that in those early days, I allowed the word of God to inspire me. I am also glad that I did not allow the enemy to use people to destroy the seed of ministry that had been planted within the depths of my soul.

We must always be careful what we allow to take root in our spirit. Every child of God must remember that words are creative. Negative words are just as creative as positive ones. Many a ministry has never gotten off the ground because some dear child of God heard the uncomplimentary words of another, and allowed the enemy to kill the ministry as soon as the seed was planted.

When the Holy Spirit prompts us with an inspired idea, or ministry, we must learn to blanket that idea or ministerial thought with prayer and fasting. I have come to a point that I realize more than ever before, that giving life to a ministry requires prayer and fasting. A preacher can go to seminary and learn how to preach. You can learn Christian counseling at the Christian college. Your pastor may be able to give you time in the pulpit to hone your preaching skills. But until the preacher learns to fast and pray for the anointing, that which we are called to do will not manifest itself. Likewise, every ministry that God places within his people requires a consistent diet of prayer and fasting. It is prayer that builds spiritual muscle, and fasting that builds spiritual insight. You will need spiritual strength to build a ministry and spiritual insight to maintain it. A songbird that is greatly anointed to sing, must continue praying, and fasting that God will keep them from the enticements of secular music. The great evangelist must continue in that which brought them success, otherwise he or she may become swallowed up in their own success. Who knows how many great preachers would still be standing had they maintained their consecrated lifestyle.

As a pastor and a leader of God's people, I have learned that the enemy can sow people into a new ministry that is striving to develop. Jesus called these type of people ravening wolves dressed in sheep's clothing. Many times they are people who we may believe to be seasoned men and women of God. New pastors may initially view them as God sent because they often bring drive, initiative and financial support. But, I encourage every new pastor to "know them that labor among you...," even as the people of God must get to know you. There are some people that may, over the course of time, do you more harm than good. I believe that through prayer and fasting, God will reveal those who may be used to cause your ministry to fail to develop. The Apostle John said in his First General Epistle "They went out from us, but they were not of us; for if they had been of us, they would no doubt have continued with us: but they went out, that they might be made manifest that they were not all of us.." Many will come and some will leave a new and striving ministry. Don't worry about those who leave, but attend to the needs of those who stay, for they make up the true embryo; help them to develop. One preacher, while giving me a word of encouragement during the early years of our ministry, told me, "God told you to feed the sheep and the lambs, but starve the goats." In other words don't spend all of your time worrying about the goats. Just feed the sheep. Many a church has failed to develop because some pastor has worried or paid to close attention to the goats, who eventually will sap all of your strength and leave you unable to effectively minister to the sheep. In addition, your church or individual ministry can fail to develop or worse abort itself in its infancy, if you pay too close attention to negative comments and questions by people who have not your vision. Remember, when God gives you a vision for your life, it is the vision He has given you. And while some others may mean well they may not be able to see your vision, because it was not given to them. Whenever someone comments negatively about what I feel God has given me, I evaluate that comment based on certain criteria. First I ask myself the question; do I know that the vision was from God? Second, I ask has God confirmed that vision? Next I ask, has God been blessing me to move toward the fulfillment of my vision? If my answers are positive, I can feel relatively safe in discounting the negative comments of others. You might ask, why would I go through this evaluation if I know God has given me a vision for my life. My answer is simple; anyone can miss the mind of God. And no matter what, every child of God should always want to be in the perfect will of God. If God should send you a messenger to help clarify His purpose for your life, you must be open enough to receive what God is saying, but you must be sure it is God. Additionally, if you are being Spirit led, you will be able to give spiritual witness of a Rhema word for your life. More than anything else, your ministry can spontaneously abort itself when you fail to care for it. It is just like in the natural, if you do not care for yourself the chance of spontaneous abortion is increased. Any doctor will tell you, that the mother who is in better physical condition has the best chance of bringing her child to birth. Every child of God must take care to nurture themselves spiritually if you intend to bring forth fruit for God. In addition, if you do not care for your ministry, it may die within you. You must nurture your ministry. Feed your ministry with the word of God as it relates to what God has called you to do. And always keep your ministry on the altar before the Lord. This is the one sure way of allowing the fire of ministry to continue burning within your soul.

Second Tri-Mester

"But we have this treasure in earthen vessels, that the Excellency of the power may be of God, and not of us."

II Corinthians 4:7

Abortion Of A Ministry, By Choice

There are at least four ways in which a ministry can die. It can die by DECEPTION, it can die by and through ERROR, it can die by the LACK OF NOURISHMENT or it can die by CHOICE. When a ministry dies by deception, it dies because someone or something is sown into it by the enemy. For instance an erroneous doctrine can cause the death of a ministry. A prophecy "so called" by a lying spirit, imposed upon a weak saint or saints can cause one to turn from that which God has called them. An unwise opinion, not in line with the WORD God had originally given you, can cause the untimely death of your ministry. We must be careful to guard the vision and inspiration that God has given us for whatever the ministry that He has planted within. We must be mindful also that every opinion will not be an erroneous one, but we must learn to sift through the rubble. We must learn to carefully and prayerfully consider the words and or opinions of others, laying them before the Lord before acting in behalf of or against them.

The second way a ministry can die is by error. Error comes when we make a mistake in either hearing from God, moving with God; moving too slow or not at all. I preached a message on one occasion about the law of timing. I believe that everything we will ever do in God will be based upon His time schedule and not ours. The writer of the book of Ecclesiastes stated under the inspiration of God; that *"To everything there is a season, and a time to every purpose under the heaven", Eccl. 3:1.* I believe God has specific times for specific things to come to fruition in our lives. But as is customary in God's dealing with us, He gives us a choice to either follow His plan or not. There have been many people who have heard from God, they know what God's message is to them, they know what God's ministry is for them, but have been afraid to move at the appointed time. Many have spent countless hours seeking multiple signs and have missed the time of the move of God's spirit for their growth. Signs and confirmations are good, but when its time to move we must move. The greatest movement by God in your area of ministry will not come randomly but at the time and season appointed by God for you. One of the worst things you can do is miss your season. The other is to move into ministry before God's appointed time. It is a terrible thing to be in the right place at the wrong time. At that point we are doing the work of God, in the place of God but God's hand or his anointing upon the work is not there yet. Remember the word of the Lord recorded in the book of Habakkuk chapter 2 verse 3; *"For the vision is yet for <u>an appointed time</u>, but at the end it shall speak, and not lie: though it tarry, <u>wait for it</u>; because it will surely come, <u>it will not tarry</u>."* If you move into ministry before it occurs or before the time, your struggle will be greater than necessary. It may be more than you can handle and ultimately destroy the work. Strive to make sure that when you move it is truly your time. We must learn the signs of the move of God in our lives. We must know when the hand of God is upon us for good. As a layperson this does not mean that every time you feel the hand of God, you must move to another church and work in a new ministry. As a layperson you must realize that many times when God places His hand upon you, and you feel an extra push in the spirit, this is an indicator of elevation and multiplied blessings in the church where you attend. It is at that point that one should become more watchful for the Lord to make opportunities for you to be used in areas of ministry not previously opened to you.

The next way a ministry can die is by lack of nourishment. In the natural birthing of a child, lack of nourishment occurs when the mother does not properly care for herself; therefore her unborn child is not properly fed. You and I must always take care of ourselves spiritually. We cannot be fully used of God if we are spiritually under-nourished. To feed a ministry, you must be properly fed. You must have something to give a ministry and enough in you to keep you in the ministry through tough times. To be properly nourished a person must have a love for the word of God. It is the word of God that will keep you, stabilize you and establish you. A shout will give you joy, but the word of God is your foundation. It will stabilize you when the going gets rough. It will secure you when others doubt and it will refresh you through your wilderness journey. In the spirit, as in the natural, you must be tapped into the source of life. Everyone needs a healthy prayer life. Being in communication with God is essential to the development of both you and your ministry. If you are in touch with God, you can never go wrong. Your ministry can never die if you are hooked into the source of its life. You will never be at a loss for direction as long as you are in constant contact with God. Remember the Bible says; *"The steps of a good man are ordered "or directed' by the Lord..." Psalm 37:23.* I have also found that it is in your best interest to have a prayer partner as you strive to develop your ministry. Having a prayer partner gives you someone not only to pray with you, but someone to help lift and encourage you through times of testing and struggle. In the natural birthing process, there is nothing like a good birthing coach. In the spiritual, there is nothing like having someone praying for you, who has a heart for you and the work that God is doing in your life. There may be some times when that person will be the one God will use to get you to continue pushing when you feel like giving up.

But alas, when a ministry dies by choice, it dies because the vessel that is to carry the ministry gives up on it. This is characterized in the story of the sower who sowed seed on stony ground. The Bible says in St. Matthew chapter 13 that a sower went forth to sow; and he sowed in four different places. One of the places he sowed seed was in stony places. This is where I want to draw your attention. The stony places can be characterized as the individuals who receive God's word concerning their ministry with joy. And they endure for a while; they go through the beginning stages of development. They are fired up initially, but after a while of enduring, after a while of suffering, when affliction and persecution ariseth, when they have been talked about too much; when they have heard too many unbelieving opinions; when they feel that its taking too long to bring the vision to maturity; when they feel that the fruit has not grown quickly enough for their standards or the standards of others, they are offended. Simply put, they give up. Someone once told me a story of a man who went on a camping trip. While walking through the woods and enjoying the scenery, he realized that he had lost his sense of direction and did not know where he was. He feverously walked in every direction trying to find his way. As nightfall came upon him, cold and hungry, he resolved it in his mind that he would never see home and never be able to find his way. He sat down and wrote a letter to his wife and children, letting them know how much he loved them and how sorry he was that he would never see them again. Tearfully he stuffed the letter inside his jacket, curled up in a ball and went to sleep. Two days later his body was found fifty feet from the main highway, which had been closed for the night. And the moral of the story is: whatever you do, don't give up, especially when things seem extremely tough. The last moments of birth, just before the child is to come forth often are the toughest, but afterward they yield the most joy. When in the toughest of times, you must speak to your vision and declare that by the power of the Spirit of God it shall come to fruition. Rather than give up we must learn to affirm the promises of God in our life. We must learn to speak life through the Word of God. The Bible declares unto us in Galatians chapter 6 and verse 9; *"And let us not be weary in well doing: for in due season we shall reap, if we faint not…"*. The provision is there for you. The reward awaits you. The requirement is, you must not faint, you must not quit. Abortion in the natural occurs when for whatever reason the mother decides that she can not handle the responsibility and she feels that there is no other way out. In the spirit we know that we can do all things through Christ who gives us strength. In the spirit we know that when we are weak God is strong. In the spirit we realize that the grace of God is sufficient for us because His strength is perfected in us in our own weakness. Never give up the vision that God has placed in your spirit for in due season it will manifest itself in you. "For the vision is yet for an appointed time,… though it tarry wait for it; because it will surely come,…".

Are You Ready To Carry Your Ministry

One of the biggest decisions you will ever make in God, is the decision to move forward into the area of ministry that He has chosen for you. Every successful person knows that before you can embrace your success, you must first make a decision. Nothing is possible until you make up your mind to do something. I once preached a message titled, "There's A Story Behind My Glory". In this message I tried to bring those in the audience to an awareness of the fact that there are a great many elements that go into the story that must be written about our life, as we journey toward successful ministry in God. The Bible says in Romans 8:28, that all things work together for good to them who love God, and who are the called according to His purpose. There are a great many life experiences that go into the making of a ministry. Many people will cross your path as you move toward full usefulness in God. Each person you meet, each experience you have, each ordeal you go through, every test, and every trial are all the building blocks that will eventually give your ministry the strength required to make it successful. A good pastor will need a good dose of humility. Humility however, comes through humbling experiences. If one is to develop compassion for souls, God will undoubtedly take this individual through certain experiences that will help develop within you the compassion necessary for ministry. If one is to be used mightily in the ministry of healing, God will at some point in time develop within you a burden for those who are sick and in need of healing. For this individual just walking through the halls of a hospital will be a moving experience. You may at some point feel an overwhelming need to minister every time you visit a sick ward. Whatever the ministry, be assured that God will over time properly prepare you for it. Even your secular employment will be used by God to prepare you for ministry. I remember leaving the graphics field, after having been an artist for more than fifteen years. I felt an overwhelming desire to work in an area that would allow me to have more one on one interaction with people. As an artist, I dealt with a particular, set group of people on an everyday basis. God in his wisdom inspired me to move into the sales arena. As a salesperson, I would have to deal with a variety of people and situations. I began working in retail sales and sold stereos, televisions and VCR's. This constant interaction with such a wide variety of people; from different ethnic backgrounds, nationalities and economic levels, was how God began teaching me how to deal with all kinds of people. Later God moved me into automobile sales where I learned how to be honest and compassionate, not allowing money to become more important than my reputation as a man of God. Later in corporate printing sales, I learned how to make a plan, work a plan and see a project through to the end. God even used my employer to help me become a better public speaker by sending me to Dale Carnagie training. I will never forget that prior to attending Dale Carnagie training I almost never felt comfortable being called to speak at the last minute. I would almost never speak publicly without a manuscript. After my training I was able to speak with or without a manuscript; and with or without notes. Being called to speak at the last minute has never been as much of a problem as it once was. Sure, there are still some nerves associated with speaking in front of a large audience but my level of comfort has greatly increased.

I am a firm believer that whatever God has called you to do he will properly prepare you to do it. The first lines of a sermon I preached entitled "The Making Of You" says that "God uses people, circumstances and time to bring you to full maturity in him. One might ask, what does all of this have to do with carrying your ministry? My answer is simply this, when a woman carries a child her body goes through changes. These changes are necessary for several reasons. Number one, a woman's body must change to accommodate the growth of the child she is carrying. It must also change so that the child might be properly nourished while developing in the womb. A woman's body must change so that when the child is born, she will be able to nurture or feed the newborn child. I believe a woman's sensitivity to her child begins developing while she is carrying her baby. Likewise, when you begin to carry your baby "ministry" you will go through several changes. These changes will help the ministry develop within you. They will also prepare you to nurture the ministry as it develops within you and after it is born. While your ministry is developing within your spirit, you must be prepared to nurture it. Your spirit must be prepared to feed the vision of ministry while it develops. It cannot be allowed to die for lack of nourishment. Therefore, God must work on you spiritually in every stage of your developing ministry. As a child of God, when you begin carrying your ministry, your spirit man must grow at the same rate of ministry development. Prayer is essential, fasting is essential. These two elements nurture both you and your ministry, they also keep God's ministry vision alive in your spirit.

The Struggle Of Travail

The word *travail* defined means "physical or mental work or exertion of a painful or laborious nature. The five words that have been underlined truly define the magnitude of the process many will go through on their way to a truly anointed ministry. If you are a pastor, who is beginning a "grass roots" ministry, with no real organizational backing, you will quickly be able to identity with these five words. Developing a church from the roots is physically and mentally challenging. Getting it to be all that you believe God has destined for it is summed up in the word travail. It will cost you in time, finances, energy, sleepless nights, fasting, prayer and an over abundance of faith. I believe that no amount of seminary or Bible College training can truly prepare a new pastor for developing a grass roots church with little or no organizational backing. But needless to say, with God all things are possible to those who believe. And to quote an unknown author; *"If God brought you to it, He'll bring you through it."* As long as you are operating within the program of God for your life, nothing can stop you from your appointed destiny. But, remember, no man is an island. Try to align yourself with good Bible believing ministers, people who can encourage you and help support you in your efforts. Many ministries have failed not because the leaders have not been called of God, but some have not associated themselves with the proper individuals, who could be helpful in troublesome times. A friendly breakfast; a kind word; a fellowship service or a pat on the back, "an atta boy" goes a long way when things get tough.

If you are a layperson making your way through the wilderness of anointing, remember, preparation is seventy five percent of the battle. Prior to the birthing of your ministry will come the trying or testing of your faith. But, as the scripture has said *"The trying of our faith worketh patience. But let patience have her perfect work, that ye may be perfect and entire, wanting nothing."* I referred earlier to the wilderness of anointing. The wilderness of anointing represents a period of time that you will have, wherein you may not be sure where you are going, only that you are following the leading of the Lord. This is a time of uncertainty in some areas of your life. It may be a time of discomfort. You may feel separated to some extent. If you have always been a people person and now you find yourself alone, wondering why you don't seem to have as many friends as you used to or you don't feel as comfortable with your friends, take heart, nothing is wrong with you. Many times, because of the nature of the ministry that you have, God will separate you to himself for a season. This will be a time of fasting, prayer and consecration unto God. At this time you will be able to hear from God more clearly than at any other time. However, this will not be a time of separation of oneself from church, church responsibilities, home and the care thereof. God has set certain systems within the church that work along with the calling on our lives. One of these systems is that of corporate worship and praise. Nothing replaces the corporate worship service in the life of a child of God. Your local church is the place where God has chosen to presence himself on a weekly basis. He expects those who have a shepherd to be under the authority of that shepherd. Therefore, he expects us to be faithful to the leadership that he has assigned to us. Also, several times during your wilderness anointing you will experience breakthroughs. Believe it or not, most of them will occur at church during your regular worship service. In addition, God expects every child of God to fulfill his or her earthly responsibilities as it relates to home family and employment. Unless God opens a window of finance whereby you do not have to work, you must be found faithful in attending to your employment responsibilities. Your employer will not be sympathetic to your ministerial desires taking precedence over company requirements. Be a faithful employee and a true Christian example. You will also notice; that while God is working on developing your ministry, your family will still need your attention. Your wife or husband will still need you. Your children still need the presence and attention of mommy or daddy. What must be learned is time management; knowing how to apportion time for everybody and every event of our lives. It serves no purpose in your life to arrive at an assumed destiny, with a totally dysfunctional family. The very best service you can do for God is never forget your family.

Any mother will tell you that travailing in birth is painful. But, after the travail comes the fruit of a new life. I encourage everyone who feels a call of God upon your life, to pray without ceasing. Be diligent in your efforts for God. Seek God with all of your heart, and stay before the face of God. For when Zion shall travail she shall bring forth her children.

As God begins to bring you through your wilderness anointing, the word of God will be more clear in your mind. You will be more sensitive to the move of God's Spirit. Others will even begin to see a difference in the anointing on you. But it's not over yet, God has just moved you closer to where he wants you to be. You have been made ready for the next step.

THIRD TRI-MESTER

"...but this <u>one thing I do</u>, forgetting those things which are behind, and reaching forth unto those things which are before, <u>I press toward</u> the mark <u>for the prize</u> of the high calling of God in Christ Jesus."

Philippians 3:13,14

Refusing To Become Distracted

One of the easiest ways for a ministry to die is when the visionary becomes distracted. In the book of Matthew chapter 13, we learn that the place where the word of God falls determines its long-term effectiveness. This applies to a seed-vision for ministry, which is sown into our lives. In order for the vision to truly come to fruition, it must first become deeply rooted in our spirit. In the before-mentioned parable, one of the places that the word of God is planted is among the thorns. As it relates to ministry, the thorns in our lives are the cares of this life. Each and every one of us has issues or cares that must be dealt with. We cannot altogether dismiss our earthly responsibilities. Even though we are not of the world we must exist in the world. In order for us to exist in the world, we must maintain jobs. We must maintain our homes; the car must be maintained, the children must be fed, and the bills must be paid. How we manage these thorny areas will determine our long-term effectiveness and the ultimate fulfillment of our individual destiny in God. Matthew 13:22 states; *"He also that received seed among the thorns is he that heareth the word; and the care of this world, and the deceitfulness of riches, choke the word, and he becometh unfruitful."* When God sows a seed-vision into our lives, he also empowers us to manage the thorny areas. God empowers us to not only come to a place of maturity in our area of ministry, but, he expects us to grow in the natural managing of our everyday lives. If everyday life management is out of order, it will be difficult for us to work effectively in ministry. A minister who has a chaotic home life, will have a chaotic ministry. Their ministry will be ineffective because there is no order to their natural lives. A person who has the ministry of intercessory prayer must properly manage every aspect of their life. An effective intercessory prayer ministry requires carefully planned prayer hours. If you have a job and a family, you will have to properly manage your day to give you enough quality time with God. Many of the distractions that kill a ministry are those areas of daily living that are not properly managed. There have been many ministries that have also died due to lack of focus. As a young man I always liked watching horse races. Because of my stature, I had even considered becoming a jockey. As a young man, I would sit around the television watching the harness races. I noticed that the horses had a leather shield on both sides of its face which shielded its eyes. The shield keeps the horse from becoming distracted by things going on around it. Therefore the horse's eyes are always fixed on the race ahead. If God has called you to a ministry, you need to put on your spiritual blinders, and get focused. A ministry can never come to fruition, when the person with the seed-vision, is distracted by things going on around them. Many small grass roots church ministries have died because the minister became distracted by the greatness of the ministry around the corner or down the street. Remember if you as a minister are distracted by what others are doing, those who you try to lead will become distracted by it also. If your ministry is within the ministry of a local church, whether you are a youth leader, missionary, prayer warrior usher or choir director, you must keep focused on your youth group, your mission, your prayer group, your usher board, and your choir. Always keep in mind that your enthusiasm or lack thereof will be passed on to those you lead. Put your spiritual blinders on and keep them on. Keep your eyes on the goals that God has placed within your spirit. Additionally, someone who is multi-talented can very quickly become a jack-of-all-trades and a master of none in the church. Or, you can be spread so thin with multiple jobs that the area which should be your area of focus becomes just one of the many jobs that does not get your full attention. Be prayerful in accepting multiple jobs so that you will not lose your zeal or effectiveness in ministry. This however, may be difficult if you are a member of a small fellowship. At small fellowship churches, it is often necessary for a few people to do multiple jobs to ensure successful ministry. This however should only be for the short term. And as the ministry grows, learn to be eager and willing to let others take over some of the areas that you have been working in. This will free you up to fulfill your destiny in the area of your specific calling. The pastor who starts up a grass roots or new ministry will also have to learn to give up certain responsibilities as the ministry begins to grow. I know from personal experience, that as a ministry grows it is easy for the pastor to continue doing multiple jobs, even though there may be others capable of fulfilling those responsibilities. By allowing others to handle some of the responsibilities such as counseling, hospital visits, van service and church administration. The pastor then creates an atmosphere for the people to grow, and also frees himself to focus on other areas of ministry that will enable him or her to grow as a minister. He will also make it possible for the ministry to grow holistically at a more rapid rate. This will allow those who have expertise in these areas to become useful in the work of the ministry. You would be surprised as to how much better your ministry will function when you are surrounded with and utilize people who have expertise in ministry.

As I considered natural childbirth I noticed something very interesting. When a woman is about to give birth there are several things that need to take place to make the birth go as smooth as possible. First, the mother, will be totally focused on the task at hand. At the time of birth the mother is almost never concerned about peripheral issues. The only thing that is important to her is the birthing of her child. There is no thought of going shopping, or preparing food for dinner, or even a concern about other children who may be at home. There is no thought of how she looks, putting on makeup or getting her hair done. The sweat dripping from her face is of no consequence; it doesn't matter. She is not even considering the baby's name at this point. The only important issue on her mind is bringing this new life into the world. Secondly everyone who she is surrounded by are of the same mind. The Doctor, the Midwife, the Nurse, her Husband or any other attendants are all focused on her and the birthing of her baby. This brings us to two very important facts. One, you must be totally focused on your ministry or your area of ministry to successfully bring it into existence. If you are not focused you will have a hard time giving birth to your ministry. Number two, everyone who is going to be a part of or help you with your ministry must be focused on what you are doing and have your best interest at heart. If those who are supposedly helping you have alternate agendas they may ultimately hurt you and not help you. They may also cause you to be distracted as you may become swallowed up in their program, their vision and not yours. This is not to say that you should not be a part of another's plan or ministry. What it does mean is that when it's their turn for the light or focus to be on them, help them in every way possible. But, when it is your turn stay focused on your goal. Remember, one of the biggest reasons why we fail at ministry is lack of focus.

Knowing When To Push

In natural childbirth one of the most; if not the most strenuous parts of childbirth is the time spent pushing the child from the mother's womb. In my observation of this process, the mother will have to push at certain intervals. In the natural birthing the mother must push or press with all her strength in an effort to give birth. Even though the mother may be tired to the point of exhaustion, if she expects to birth her child she must continue to PUSH. Sometimes in pushing it may seem that the agony of birthing will never be brought to a conclusion. This is a time of great tension, strain and struggle. Seldom is the birth so easy that the mother does not have to labor and push the baby from her womb. At this stage she uses all of her strength, all of her mental fortitude, as she presses toward the climactic moment of childbirth. And the doctor or midwife will encourage her at the proper moment with just one word, PUSH. And so it is in the spirit. At the proper moment in time we must PUSH. Knowing when to push is simply about knowing or being sensitive to the move of God in your life. You may notice that there are times in your life when it seems that everything will go right. Everything works for you. It may seem that you couldn't mess up if you tried with all of your might and strength. People will be placed in your pathway to help you. The anointing upon you will be greater than it had been in the past. Often this is when God is positioning you to begin your push. But here is the paradoxical aspect of this time in your life. As much as everything seems to be positioned for your forward move, this may however, be the most difficult time - the time when you are going from one level to the next. The time of the birthing of the greatness that lay within you and the establishment of your ministry.

When we were about to build our new church sanctuary, we experienced the reality of this paradoxical time. On the one hand, we had obtained all of the financing we needed. The architect was in place. We had a builder who believed in our project to the point that he put up thousands of dollars of his own money to insure that our project got an early start. Donations were coming in from the left and the right. We had more chairs donated to us than we could use. We ultimately sent many of the chairs to a church in South Carolina. We received so much fiberglass insulation that we gave away enough to fully insulate another church. Someone donated a piano, someone else donated a keyboard. We received discounts for labor on our concrete work and our handicap parking was donated. Everything was working in our favor. What was the problem? The adversary had set his forces against us. He knew what we were doing would be a blessing to the kingdom of God and he was determined to stop our progress. A lot of our membership left us. Tithing went down and people began talking negative. We had to move our services to several different places. In one place we often would find ourselves locked out because the person who was responsible for opening the doors for us had either forgotten or just failed to show up. We arrived at one rented location on Palm Sunday only to find out that the facility we were renting had no chairs for us to sit on. In the midst of this I was reminded of Nehemiah and the building of the walls. God was with Nehemiah. The king was with him. He had the material to build with. But somewhere in the midst of building the enemy began to fight against him. It got so bad that the people of God had to keep their weapons of war close to their side as they pressed forward to finish the work. Discouragement set in among the people. But with his mind made up, Nehemiah realized that if the vision would ever come to fruition he had to PUSH. He had to be focused on the positive aspects of what God was doing and not get side-tracked by the devices of the enemy. This was the time when he had to press his way toward the goal that was set before him. Many were the days and nights that I would gather the men of our church and go to our shell of a building to work. I would often inspire and encourage our people to continue laboring and building the house of God. I had a goal in mind in the spirit and I was determined that I would not be denied. No obstacle would be enough to stop our forward progress. One by one we conquered. And, one by one we overcame every obstacle.

There are two aspects of PUSH that you must keep in mind when moving toward ministry birth. The first aspect is prayer. Someone broke down the word push and described it this way; Pray, Until, Something Happens. When you are at the point of birth you must pray all the more. The Bible instructs us to pray without ceasing. If ever there was a time to pray it is when you are at the point of birth. In the natural it is a very critical time for child and mother. In the spirit it is a very critical time for you and your ministry. Both you and your ministry can suffer great loss at this point in time. When everything seems to be going perfect, don't allow yourself to be lulled to sleep concerning prayer. This is the time when you need to pray all the more. When things are going right, we must remember that we still have an unseen enemy lurking in the shadows looking for a weak-spot and a way to defeat the program of God in our life. You must pray earnestly until the ministry is fully born. Pray until you break through. And remember, the devil is a master strategist. He knows exactly what to do to get us out of our spiritual game plan. Perhaps he will use a family situation, or issues on our job. He might use a disagreement at the church where your blessing is coming from or with the person from that same church that is intricately tied to your destiny. Remember, it was an issue concerning John Mark that caused Paul and Barnabas to sever their ties for a season, even though God had ordained that the two of them minister as a team. The Bible very clearly stated concerning Paul and Barnabas in Acts chapter 13 and verse 2 that; *"As they ministered to the Lord, and fasted, the Holy Ghost said, Separate me Barnabas and Saul for the work whereunto I have called them."* The devil does not care who he uses or what he uses to accomplish his goals. The only thing he is concerned about is results. We must always be cognizant of the fact that not only is Satan walking about as a roaring lion seeking whom he may devour but he is also looking to see how he can destroy ministries. We are therefore admonished to be wise, vigilant and of a clear mind concerning the tricks and tactics of the enemy. The second aspect is faith. Faith says, that I do not simply praise God after He's finished the work. I don't just wait until I see the victory. I praise God in advance of what he has promised to do. Praise God until victory is visualized in the natural. Praise God until the intangible becomes tangible. Praising God in the midst of the press will continuously invigorate, inspire, and encourage you as well as everyone associated with your ministry vision. There is no substitute for faith-based praise. The praise that says; it hasn't manifested itself in the natural but God said it, I believe it, I see it in the spirit, I embrace it by faith and I praise God now in expectation of victory. As a woman travailing in birth you must get it made up in your mind, that at every point of opposition you must PUSH. At every moment of doubt thrown your way by the enemy you must PUSH. Whenever you feel tired you must PUSH. Whenever you feel discouraged you must PUSH. Through the long hours of work and study you must PUSH. You're at the point of birth, and you must PUSH. There will be plenty of time for resting when you have finished in the birthing room, but for now you must PUSH. You have everything you need at your disposal. You've been praying, you've been fasting, the anointing on your life is at an all time high, there is a glow about you in the spirit that has not been seen before; all you have to do now is PUSH. The Bible says that to everything there is a season and a time to every purpose under the heavens. If you feel the awesomeness of the move of the spirit of God upon your ministry, you must travail like never before. Remember, seasons come and seasons go. Don't miss your season. Don't let the time of your birthing come and go leaving you with a feeling of emptiness and unfruitfulness, PUSH.

Birth Of A Ministry

No time will be greater for you than the day you look up and realize that God has brought your ministry to a level of perfection in Him. It is the joy that fulfillment in Christ brings. It is also the joy found in the recognition by ones peers that your ministry has been made full. God has brought you through many different transitional phases on your way to greater usefulness in Christ. There is no greater joy than to know that you have discovered the purpose God had intended for your life, and with it the realization that by allowing God to mold and shape you, you've now broken through to become a jewel in God's crown. Through test and trials you have now birthed a ministry that makes every thing you do in life more meaningful. This is the place for which all mankind strives. Whether we know it or not, every man goes through his or her life with a desire to know what they were created for. Because of the way God made us, no man will ever be satisfied until he or she functions according to the purpose for which they were designed. Someone once said, "A man is, what a man does." No statement could have been truer. If you do what you were designed to do, then at some point in time you will become one with the thing that you do. When you become one with the thing that you do, you will then be able to function with a level of excellence that will get the attention of everyone you come in contact with. As I have stated in the preceding chapters, getting to this level of excellence is a process. There will be ups and downs, highs and lows. But, after you have pressed your way through it all you will have arrived at a level of anointing that only time and experience with God can bring you to. If you are a pastor developing a church, there is no greater feeling than to have started with nothing and made it something worthy in the kingdom of God. If you are an Evangelist or Revivalist, when you stand before God's people and see the multitude coming to God to be saved and delivered, all the times of suffering and going without will be just a faded memory in the back of your mind as you embrace the reality of the present anointing. Nothing will compare with the joy that is before you. You will then realize that everything you had to go through to get you to this moment in time was well worth it. Every sacrifice, every pain, every press, every struggle, have all made you the person you are today.

Now that you have endured, pressed, and pushed,

your ministry has been birthed, but it's not over. Now you must be about the business of further developing and building on that which has been born. If you remain at the birthing table your ministry child will ultimately die for lack of nourishment. Feed your ministry a healthy diet of prayer, fasting, research and study. Never stop building on that which God has done in your life. Surround yourself with people that will help you to continue to develop. Search out people who are above you and working in the same ministry as yourself. Remember the baby eagle that is born ultimately depends on the adult eagle to help it learn how to fly, and not only fly but soar above the clouds. Always remember, those who have gone on before you are usually best able to help you learn how to stabilize and strengthen your wings. And the Bible says; "But the God of all grace, who hath called us unto his eternal glory by Christ Jesus, after that ye have suffered a while, make you perfect, stablish, strength, settle you." Going through the process of birthing a ministry is not easy. Giving birth to an anointed ministry is not easy. But, the joy that follows the birth will bring with an unimaginable richness to the rest of your life.

About The Author

Through wisdom is an house builded; and by understanding it is established: And by knowledge shall the chambers be filled with all precious and pleasant riches"

Proverbs 24:3,4

ABOUT THE AUTHOR

Pastor Edward Wilson gave his life to the Lord and was baptized in Jesus Name and filled with the Holy Spirit in December of 1981 at Pentecostal Bridegroom Church. Not long afterward, he began serving in the church as, Assistant Secretary of the Men's Fellowship. Later he served as its Secretary, Vice President, and President. He also served as Assistant Secretary for the State Brotherhood (Men's Fellowship) of the Pentecostal Assemblies of the World, Inc.. He received his call to the ministry in 1985 and began working as a lay minister under the late District Elder George Mayfield and later under Bishop Ronald L. Young.

Pastor Wilson attended Aenon Bible College and in 1990 was licensed as a minister in the Pentecostal Assemblies of the World. As a licensed minister, Elder Wilson served as a Supervisory Associate Minister at Pentecostal Bridegroom Temple. In this capacity Elder Wilson was responsible for guiding the executive decisions of the President of the Men's Ministry, Youth Ministry and Outreach Ministry. Elder Wilson was ordained as Founder and Pastor of Living Word Ministries, in 1992 by Bishop

Liston Page Sr. of Greater Highway Deliverance Churches, Incorporated. Elder Wilson served as the Director of Church Financial Development for the Greater Highway Deliverance Churches Inc..

Pastor Wilson is also a member of the Association of Business Leaders and Entrepreneurs [A.B.L.E.]. A.B.L.E. is a community based organization in Sicklerville, New Jersey. Founded by Mr. Bobby Harris; they are dedicated to providing support for the youth of Winslow and Monroe Townships through educational programs and college scholarships. He is also the founder of Finest of the Wheat Christian Academy.

Pastor Wilson is the author of three books, "Understanding the Pentecostal Apostolic Message", "Sermons from an Apostolic Pulpit" and "Giving Birth to an Anointed Ministry". Pastor Wilson was ordained a Bishop in the Tabernacle Of Praise Pentecostal Churches in 2005. He is married to Sister Ann Wilson who is an anointed and dedicated woman of God. Their twenty four years and counting marriage has been truly blessed by God. Together they have been richly blessed with one daughter Amber Nicole, who helps them in the ministry. As the Pastor of Mt. Zion Pentecostal Church, Pastor Wilson leads the congregation that God has given him, in a constant search for truth. Pastor Wilson is a consummate motivator. He has the unique ability of being able to see the sunshine in every dark cloud. He always encourages those who attend Mt. Zion to strive to be better and fulfill their individual destinies and the corporate destiny of the church of God. At Mt. Zion there is no such place as a comfort zone. Pastor Wilson constantly encourages everyone to expand their horizons and grow beyond their own boarders. This Pastor Wilson's third book will truly inspire and encourage everyone who reads it.

www.ingramcontent.com/pod-product-compliance
Lightning Source LLC
Chambersburg PA
CBHW031333040426
42443CB00005B/325

9780615180151